For Sonny with love
– C. H.

For Puma, my late beloved cat
– N. A.

MAGIC CAT PUBLISHING

The Elephant and the Piano © 2025 Magic Cat Publishing Ltd
Text © 2025 Colette Hiller
Illustrations © 2025 Nabila Adani

First published in 2025 by Magic Cat Publishing Ltd, an imprint of Lucky Cat Publishing Ltd,
Unit 2 Empress Works, 24 Grove Passage, London E2 9FQ, UK
EU Authorised Representative Magic Cat Publishing, an imprint of Lucky Cat Publishing Ltd,
PAKTA svetovanje d.o.o., Stegne 33, Ljubljana, Slovenia

The right of Colette Hiller to be identified as the author and Nabila Adani to be indentified
as the illustrator of this work has been asserted by her in accordance with the Copyright,
Designs and Patents Act, 1988 (UK).

No part of this publication may be reproduced, stored in a retrieval system,
or transmitted, in any form, or by any means, electrical, mechanical, photocopying,
recording or otherwise without the prior written permission of the publisher
or a licence permitting restricted copying.

A catalogue record for this book is available from the British Library.

ISBN 978-1-917044-06-6

The illustrations were created gouache, watercolor, oil pastel and digital media
Set in Neuzeit Grotesk, Canvas Script and Farmhand Sans

Published by Katie Cotton
Edited by Katie Cotton and Polly Whybrow
Designed by Stephanie Jones and Riko Sekiguchi

Manufactured in China

1 3 5 7 9 8 6 4 2

MIX
Paper | Supporting
responsible forestry
FSC® C104723

Colette Hiller · Nabila Adani

The ELEPHANT and the PIANO

Some stories are true. Others are make-believe.
And some stories are so amazing that it seems they must
be make-believe, and yet they really happened.

This is one of those stories.

In faraway Thailand, on the banks of the River Kwai, is an elephant sanctuary – a kind of paradise for elephants in need of a home. There are emerald forests where they can roam and sparkling rivers to splash in.

The elephants are well looked after and are all very happy there...

But once, there was one who wasn't.

Now, Bonti was different to the other elephants.
He didn't like playing with them,

or joining for mountain walks.

He was unpredictable and quick to get angry. He was also very big.

Everyone learned to keep their distance.

One day, a visitor called Paul was watching Bonti from behind a banana tree.

Bonti was wearing what looked like an old straw sunhat. In fact, he'd plonked a big clump of mud and grass on his head to keep off the heat (elephants do that sometimes).

When Paul looked at Bonti, he didn't see a dangerous animal, just a lonely one. He wanted to tell him he was loved, but how? Elephants don't understand human words. What if he could speak to Bonti in a different way?

Suddenly, Paul knew what to do! "Bonti," he called. "I think I can help you. If they'll let me."

With no time to lose, Paul hurried down the mountain to find the director of the sanctuary.

"I have an idea," said Paul. "It's a little bit unusual, I know... I'd like to play the piano for Bonti."

"The piano?" said the director, weakly. "But he might smash it to smithereens! It's a big risk."

"I'll take it," said Paul, and with that he zoomed off.

That night, Paul was excited but nervous.
Imagine hearing music for the very first time.
What should he play?

And then he found the perfect piece.
It was powerful yet gentle and beautiful.
"Just like Bonti," thought Paul.

The next morning, Paul's neighbours helped load the piano into an old van,

and off he set.

Bonti was by the riverbank, tucking into a pile of bana grass. He was too busy eating to notice Paul quietly setting up the piano.

Paul sat down then looked up...

Bonti towered over him.

Paul took a deep breath.
"Hello Bonti," he said.

"This piece of music is by a
human composer called Beethoven.
I thought you might like to hear it."

Then, after a few minutes, he began to sway, just slightly at first, shifting his great weight and swinging his head.

When the melody soared,
Bonti stretched his trunk high in the air.

Just at that moment, a small elephant appeared. He was trundling happily down the mountain path, making a beeline straight for Bonti!

Paul was alarmed. One swipe of Bonti's trunk could knock out the little elephant.

The little one gave Bonti a playful nudge.

Then a big push.

But Bonti didn't lash out.

And when the smaller one stepped up to the piano and dropped his trunk onto the keys with a PLINK, Bonti was curious and did the same on the other side. PLONK!

PLINK! PLONK! PLINK!

Soon they were plinking and plonking as Paul was **PLONK** playing and there was hardly any room **PLINK** for Paul's hands **PLONK!**

Afterwards the little elephant wandered off for some lunch, but Bonti stayed put, watching Paul.

"I'm glad you liked the music," he said.
"I'll be back tomorrow, I promise."

But the next day was blisteringly hot. The kind of tropical heat that hits you like an oven. It was too hot to be out in the sun – the evening would be cooler.

As he had some time, Paul set about making a special elephant piano for Bonti with an old keyboard and some wood. That way they could both play.

When Paul reached the riverbank that evening, he found his piano in its spot by the rock. Next to it, there stood Bonti, waiting.

"I'm sorry to be late," said Paul,
setting up the special elephant piano.

As the music floated up into the air, Bonti shifted and swayed. He made delicate shapes with his trunk and circles on the ground with his foot.

Just as he was taking a neat little sidestep, there was a sudden blast of trumpeting.

And then the ground began to shake.

Down the mountain they came – in single file and twos and threes. Big elephants, small elephants, mothers and babies, trumpeting and squeaking with excitement, curious to find the source of the sound.

Ears flapping, tails wagging, they gathered by the piano like party guests ready for fun.

Soon, the whole place was jumping. Except it wasn't really because elephants can't jump. But they were rocking and the little ones were rolling.

Bonti and another elephant were jamming **PLINK** on the elephant piano **PLONK** and everyone was moving **PLINK**.

The moon shone down and Paul kept playing... until it was way past everybody's bedtime.

And that's what happened when the elephants heard the piano.

But that's not really the end of the story.
For Paul still plays piano for the elephants.
To this very day.

And how they love hearing him play.

THE REAL STORY THIS BOOK IS BASED ON...

This book is about Paul Barton, an Englishman who lives in Thailand with his family. It's also about Bonti, a lonely elephant who found joy in piano music. While Paul is a real person, Bonti is based on three different elephants Paul came to know and love: Chaichana, a dangerous but sensitive bull elephant; Romsai, who especially loved Beethoven; and Plara, who almost danced in response to the music. Bonti has qualities of each!

It started in 2011 when Paul first visited a sanctuary called Elephants World. There, he met Romsai, the older elephant who, like Bonti, seemed sad and withdrawn. Paul wondered if music might help him feel better... And, it turns out, it did! He began to play more often for Romsai, seeing a change in his behaviour over time.

Since then, Paul has played piano for many elephants, getting to know several over the years. His YouTube videos have touched millions across the world and there is even an award-winning documentary, *Music for Elephants* (which this author heartily recommends).

"Beautiful music is like a language without words," Paul explains. "Just as it can lift our spirits, it can do the same for elephants." Some express themselves in movement, while others enjoy a bit of jamming.

For Paul, playing piano for elephants remains a privilege. "The best thing is when you can help an elephant like Bonti, who really connects with the music. When that happens, there's nothing more wonderful."

YOU CAN DO WHAT PAUL DOES!

You may not have a pet elephant, but did you know that cats and dogs can also enjoy a bit of music? Soothing sounds may help them relax and unwind. If you play an instrument, try starting with something gentle. Or you could sing a lullaby. Watch what happens – do they seem to enjoy it? Does it make them sleepy? Be sure they're free to walk off if they want to. (And if they do, don't be offended, you can try another time!)

HELPING ELEPHANTS WITH THIS BOOK

The author has made a donation to Phuket Elephant Jungle Sanctuary.